Best
Friends
Forever

OTHER TITLES FROM THE EMMA PRESS

POETRY ANTHOLOGIES

The Emma Press Anthology of the Sea
This Is Not Your Final Form: Poems about Birmingham
The Emma Press Anthology of Aunts
The Emma Press Anthology of Love
Some Cannot Be Caught: The Emma Press Book of Beasts

CHILDREN'S BOOKS

Watcher of the Skies: Poems about Space and Aliens
Moon Juice, by Kate Wakeling
The Noisy Classroom, by Ieva Flamingo
The Book of Clouds, by Juris Kronbergs
Queen of Seagulls, by Rūta Briede

PROSE PAMPHLETS

Postcard Stories, by Jan Carson
First fox, by Leanne Radojkovich
The Secret Box, by Daina Tabūna
Me and My Cameras, by Malachi O'Doherty

POETRY PAMPHLETS

Dragonish, by Emma Simon
Pisanki, by Zosia Kuczyńska
Who Seemed Alive & Altogether Real, by Padraig Regan
Paisley, by Rakhshan Rizwan

THE EMMA PRESS PICKS

The Dragon and The Bomb, by Andrew Wynn Owen
Meat Songs, by Jack Nicholls
Birmingham Jazz Incarnation, by Simon Turner
Bezdelki, by Carol Rumens

BEST FRIENDS FOREVER

Poems on female friendship

Edited by Amy Key
Illustrated by Emma Wright

For my most brilliant friends

⸱℘℘⸱

'Just in case you ever foolishly forget; I'm never not
thinking of you.' Virginia Woolf, *Selected Diaries*

THE EMMA PRESS

First published in Great Britain in 2014 by the Emma Press Ltd

Poems copyright © individual copyright holders 2014
Selection and introduction copyright © Amy Key 2014
Illustrations copyright © Emma Wright 2014

The right of Amy Key to be identified as the editor of this work
has been asserted by her in accordance with the Copyright,
Designs and Patents Act 1988.

ISBN 978-1-910139-07-3

A CIP catalogue record of this book is available
from the British Library.

Printed and bound in Great Britain by Imprint Digital, Exeter.

The Emma Press
theemmapress.com
queries@theemmapress.com
Jewellery Quarter, Birmingham, UK

Contents

SOME THINGS WE BOTH KNOW

Introduction

I drew her to me

The friendships I have with women are some of the most vital in my life, and while editing this book I found myself considering how they began. Some grew through proximity or confinement: a school class, a bus journey, the nearness of desks. Others were sparked by an enchantment – a kind of falling in love with someone from afar and feeling a desperate desire to reach out and forge a friendship with them, even having to ask: 'Will you be my friend?'

We all have our choice of sisters

When I was younger, I wanted to be part of the cult of Best Friends. I wanted the necklace, the endless telephone talk and the secret pact. I wanted to be able to name the girl in that coveted spot. I wanted that certainty both emotionally (my own dear heart) and practically (someone to eat my lunch with).

Then, when I was 14, the riot grrrl movement connected me to other women and gave me a worldwide cohort of sisters. This was a massively emboldening thing for me and the idea of The One BFF became less important, as I began to understand friendships as more elastic, complex and various. While the count-on-one hand friends are steadfast and have become like sisters, there have been others who were very present in my life for just a little time – the right time – and who will always be special to me. Knowing this also makes me wonder about the friends I've not yet made, who will become important to me in future years.

I let your hand go

I think my love for my friends is a romance in itself. It has a soundtrack, special places, shared beds and toothbrushes. It has borrowed pyjamas and screaming rows, its own drunken 'I LOVE YOU' text messages and conspiratorial power. And it has its breakups.

Occasionally I wake in the night with a friend in mind, a friend whose hand I dropped without ever really meaning to. I was 17 then and I'm 36 now, but it still makes me sad. It makes me wonder if I'm a good enough friend to the women in my life now. Quite often I think I am not.

I worry social media has made me lazy, taking it for granted that my friends are okay because Facebook suggests all is well. (I know how easy it is to dress up that particular shop window.) I'm forever saying: 'I am here for you.' But am I really? I know there are times I've let friends down and shut people out, causing some friendships to fall away because I simply wasn't paying enough attention. I grieve for some friendships still, and whenever I listen to Stevie Nicks singing 'Gypsy'('she is dancing away from me now') my heart squirms, because I know that eventually I'll lose someone not through neglect or because I've messed up, but because they won't be here anymore.

The things we both know

My best friendships are founded in acute empathy, of experience, eating habits, dressing, politics. The empathy is a magic force, and I like to think a little bit of me is nested in all the friends I've made, a live or latent connection that can be activated at any time. This access to empathy

– the opportunity to love so variously and deeply, to be accepted and forgiven and inspired – is what makes my friendships with women so special to me.

೮೦೧

This book began with a hunch: that friendship between women is not well represented in contemporary poetry. I did a survey on Twitter and Facebook and found that people's favourite friendship poems were mostly written by men and dealt with brotherhood, camaraderie, war and intellectual rivalry.

Female friendship, when you can find it, tends to be portrayed in a very extreme way: either on the brink of being torn apart, with a love object getting in the way, or reduced to 'a girls' night in', all ice cream and manicures. I love ice cream and I love manicures, but they melt and chip and in no way represent the vital and sustaining relationships between good girl friends.

That this is an anthology of poems on female friendship is especially appropriate – some of the most important friendships in my life have been developed through meeting poets and writers in workshops or readings or getting to know them online.

In this collection, I've sought out poems which portray female friendships in all their jewelled variety. These relationships are not all flawless; perfection is most definitely not the point. Some are soft or brittle. Some you might sharpen yourself against. Some catch the light. Some dazzle you. Some you never take off. Some you'll never be able to.

Amy Key, October 2014

I drew her to me

The Visitation

Eloise, I opened too soon, like a foxglove, on that papered bed,
my waters sweet and grassy as the cut-side in Spring,
and cried when the little nurse drew the curtains around me

and said, 'hush wench, yo've a long night ahead' and left me
to watch the sun tumble and climb through the high gridded windows.
In the cubicles around me women were sobbing.

I lay my cheek against the cold bars of the trolley
as my body clenched and unfurled and I slept for just a moment
and in that moment I was fourteen again and still your girl,

lying on my back in the playing fields in Dudley,
my blue school skirt hitched, the unmown grass wet
against my legs; summer overspilling and everything loosened.

You knelt before me, your scent of hairspray and menthol
kaylighing my lungs and took my face in your palms,
placed a coronet of daisies in my hair and held me down

until my mouth opened upon flowers and my body bloomed flowers
red and feverish, filling the fields and gardens,
the narrow beds of girls, wild in the cots where babies slept.

I knew the time had come to yield like a meadow
so I did, love, and you moved through me like the May breeze
and I was blessed.

Will You Be My Friend, Kate Moss?

My daughter's in your daughter's ballet class.
I sat beside you at the Christmas show?
I really loved the outfit you had on!
Three years ago I tried to emulate
your look in *Grazia*: you can't believe
how hard it was to find some knee-high boots,
a tunic-dress, and earrings just like yours.
The icon of my generation, Kate,
you were The Waif – that's what we aimed to be –
and yet it's so unfair you got the blame
for all that teenage anorexia.
We'd never look like you no matter what:
I saw that when you walked into the class
(your daughter was ecstatic, by the way!)
your terrifying cheekbones mocking mine.
The line 'Alas poor Yorick' struck me then:
your head could easily be on Hamlet's palm!
And speaking of: I heard your friend Jude Law
is in New York reprising Hamlet at
the Broadhurst Theatre on 44th.
I miss New York – I wish that we could go.
I have this friend, Nuar, I'm sure you'd love:
she's smarter than the two of us combined,
and stunning, too, and has two little girls.
At Yaddo, where we met, she'd quote Foucault
and Nietzsche on the buffet line. She held
my hand one creepy night when we got lost
around the lake beside her studio.

I really miss Nuar, and Suki too,
whose sense of style is on a par with yours.
Let's all go out one night! I'll do my best
to stick with you despite the fact that I'm
a hypochondriac and petrified
of class A drugs. We have so many things
in common, like you're pretty much my age;
we share initials; the circumference of
our thighs is basically the same. (I checked.)
I also saw you surreptitiously
admire my silver space-age dress! You did!
Now that my daughter's been moved up a grade
will this be adios amigo, Kate?
She's not disconsolate about the change
but then she's at the age where all you say
is 'will you be my friend'. Remember that?

Ute

I will try to tell you about Ute; she is so complex; it is quite difficult.
She sails into the gym, swathed in scarves; red hat pulled down low,
gauntlets, olive skin, Burmese cat blue eyes behind dark glasses,
thigh-booted, and with great swooping laughs and greetings.
Her car is sporty, and in winter has pale grey furry covers,
not only on the seats, but on the steering wheel and safety belts.

It's crammed with baskets of food, jars of honey, eggs and flowers.
She always carries a fringed, hammocky bed that doubles
as her yoga mat; the whole effect has a swingy, gypsy elegance.
In action she is very good and lithe. She was once a modern dancer,
then turned to teaching yoga. She is exactly the same age
as I am, is of German origin, and has been married twice.

When the war broke out she was on holiday in the Baltic
on the family yacht. She was sent to Pomerania to avoid the bombs.
After the war, her family, military aristos, disgusted at the upstart Hitler,
moved to Hungary to start again. Her father and brother committed suicide,
the Russians invaded Hungary, and with husband, son and mother
she came to America to live down the shame and horror of it all.

She claims she knew all about the concentration camps
and the Holocaust when she was only 13. She detests social life
and never goes to parties. She prefers the company of cats,
young addicts, and devotes herself to her bed-ridden mother of 98
who does not speak a word of English. She's vestigially Catholic,
permanently Buddhist and is full of love, laughter and givingness.

Zero Balancer

for Susie

Dazzler of farm boys, Capoeira dancers,
at twenty you could turn a cartwheel
of such slow grace it was impossible
not to love you, you in your rabbit fur.
There were things you did I'd never seen
before, like buttering soft-boiled eggs,
the order of your eating, each forkful
a precise bit of everything on the plate.
You could make a dressing gown, dare
somersaults, knew the ratio of Lapsang
to Earl Grey. Where I moped untidily,
you modelled an immaculate rage.
We leant to the warmth that passes
shoulder to shoulder. Now, your fingers
are tuned to resistance. Freckle-handed,
we trump grandchildren, annuities, aches.
There's not one small bone in my body
you can't nudge back into its comfortable place.

I Want To Be In Your Gang

I want to paint my nails green with yellow tips whilst I reblog pictures of bloodstained clothing, stills from 1990s teen movies and pictures of iced cakes. Then, even when I'm sitting alone in the library or in my bedroom, I'll know that I'm not really alone.

I want to wear babydoll dresses and pink, yellow or lavender wigs as we rouge our lips red and dust our faces with marabou puffs, high kicking in time to a punk rock soundtrack as tears stream down our cheeks, mascara rainbows.

I want to ride around the city in a pink convertible with the top down and Kitty's Emobounce playing on the stereo wearing a glitter letter emblazoned denim jacket with my hair in a side ponytail with a large bow and lipstick bleeding over the corners of my lips.

I want to rollerskate around the park in a band tee and a pair of customized hightop sneakers with the wind blowing through my hair and Kreay's Summertime playing on my iPod.

I want to lounge on striped deckchairs next to a pool sipping on strawberry milkshakes in plastic cups through straws in pigtails or plaits and heart-shaped or floral-edged sunglasses, or aviators, in sunscreen, in fake tan, whilst we watch everyone.

I want to have a slumber party where we all lie around in sequinned or lamé costumes and flutter fans whilst listening to Bow Wow Wow and X-Ray Spex records.

I want to have a tea party wearing crumpled floral 1950s dresses and vintage petticoats and ripped nylons and eat cupcakes and macaroons with cream and icing and glitter and blood and guts.

The Chew

We know that nothing is never only itself:
a tomato is a gourd, a sun pulped lover
a picture of god –

and there are gods! One of them is me
another is her printing press
and you can live like this

and when I'm off my head on the grief ship
she walks me along the canal
makes room for me on the planet

or at least the tow path
so when one of us phones hammered and dumped
on the tremulous fault line

there's just merriness like Have a sherry
stay perky, stay dirty in case he thinks of you –
Oh how he thinks of you!

We fools keep each other pain-blinking
in the stew
togethering the pictures in our tomato brains.

Offchurch

The wheat is ready for cropping, a full congregation
beside the road through the fields from nowhere to dismantled nowhere,
a brick bridge over a thirsty ditch and the cedar holding up its green tray
are the only telltales that there was once a big house that went on fire
or was sold in parts like a butchered cow and sometimes,
one evening in five, a car will crawl through to a corrugated farm.

And this is the only time you took the walk with me,
and because you were there and could charm a fish out of its pond
and make it want to stand on its tail to please you:
a saucer-faced barn owl pushed out from the stag oak,
boated into the blue for a moment, then dropped down into the corn.

Hot Corona

Today I caught the sun
it wasn't hard as all that
a simple lasso did the trick
I drew her to me
and the light was blinding
I let her go awhile
and the new cold
overwhelmed me
It was difficult to maintain
a middling distance
she was so buoyant
despite her weight
and gravity was growing furious
The earth began to growl
I felt worried
but the sun did not appear to notice
She complimented my hair
and it felt like a hard scratch
I looked at her directly
and saw dark spots on her surface
like small craters
and this shocked me a bit
I asked the spoken language of her neighbourhood
and she laughed softly
without elaboration
I asked how she liked to be called
and she told me Hot Corona

I asked her about the moon
had they met etc.
and she went all dim
said nothing
The sun was highly superstitious
like all stars she said

We all have our
choice of sisters

I Wish I Had More Sisters

I wish I had more sisters,
enough to fight with and still
have plenty more to confess to,
embellishing the fight so that I
look like I'm right and then turn
all my sisters, one by one, against
my sister. One sister will be so bad
the rest of us will have a purpose
in bringing her back to where
it's good (with us) and we'll feel
useful, and she will feel loved.

Then another sister
will have a tragedy, and again
we will unite in our grief, judging
her much less that we did the bad
sister. This time it was not
our sister's fault. This time
it could have happened to any
of us and in a way it did. We'll
know she wasn't the only
sister to suffer. We all suffer
with our choices, and we
all have our choice of sisters.

My sisters will seem like a bunch
of alternate me's, all the ways
I could have gone. I could see
how things pan out without
having to do the things myself.

———————

The abortions, the divorces,
the arson, swindles, poison jelly.
But who could say they weren't
myself, we are so close. I mean,
who can tell the difference?

I could choose to be a fisherman's
wife, since I'd be able to visit
my sister in her mansion, sipping
bubbly for once, braying
to the others, who weren't invited.
I could be a traveller, a seer,
a poet, a potter, a flyswatter.
None of those choices would be
as desperate as they seem now.
My life would be like one finger
on a hand, a beautiful, usable, ringed,
wrung, piano-and-dishpan hand.

There would be both more and less
of me to have to bear. None of us
would be forced to be stronger
than we could be. Each of us could
be all of us. The pretty one.
The smart one. The bitter one.
The unaccountably-happy-
for-no-reason one. I could be,
for example, the hopeless
one, and the next day my sister
would take my place, and I would
hold her up until my arms gave way
and another sister would relieve me.

best

my best friend lost her housekeys and wallet
buying waterchestnuts in the chinese supermarket.
my best friend has a mole on her ankle
I hijacked for the eye of an elaborate biro parrot.
my best friend has been to all of the greek islands
she has been to france twice not including guernsey.

your best friend is retraining in accountancy/
has moved to leeds or was it glasgow/
has a cat you are quietly, fastidiously, allergic to.
your best friend goes to great lengths laddering
her tights before parties/ plays grade two trumpet/
is scrubbing last night's red wine off the kitchen lino.

your best friend is not having a photo taken but
is not looking my best friend is stoically fluent
in latin your best friend did two tango lessons,
intermediate dressmaking my best friend is cooking
one of hugh fearnley's recipes is substituting
table vinegar for wine even as we speak

Soup Sister

And, of course,
it bothers me greatly that I can't know
the quality of the light where you are.
How your each day pans out,
how the breeze lifts the dry leaves from the street
or how the street pulls away from the rain.

Last week I passed a tree
that was exactly you in tree form,
with a kind look and sub-branches
like your delicate wrists.

Six years ago we were lying
in a dark front room on perpendicular sofas,
so hungover that our skin hurt to touch.
How did we always manage
to be heartbroken at the same time?

I could chop, de-seed and roast
a butternut squash for dinner
in the time it took you to shower.

Steam curtained the windows, whiting out
the rain, which hit the house sideways.
One of us, though I forget who, said
do you think women are treated like bowls
waiting to be filled with soup?
And the other one said, of course.

Now the world is too big,
and it's sinking and rising
and stretching out its back bones.
The rivers are too wild,
the mountains are so so old
and it's all laid out arrogantly between us.

My friend, how long do you stand
staring at the socks in your drawer
lined up neat as buns in a bakery,
losing track of time and your place in the world,
in the (custardy light of a) morning?

Roller Girls

Chelsea's immaculate skies, the fire escape, our escape,
where we light up side by side, shine in spring, summer,

sing ditties at our desks, typing overly flamboyantly,
we lark about then leave on the dot (finally for good)

for birthdays and carnivals, always and forever dancing,
parties, sleepovers, Sundays, roller-skating round the flat

in pants, arms linked, heady, we speed through holidays,
heart aches, in place of tears, last night's glitter sparkling

on our cheeks; in Pimlico, in the shade of sainted squares,
by grand frosted terraces we promenade your pram,

stop off for blanket adjustments, fruited toast,
chat in whispery voices to lull this new fascination,

circuit-side, cheer on your love, gasp at corners taken,
fancy-dressed, face-painted, Ziggy and GaGa, dance back

to forever, at roller disco, skating hand in hand –
we were daredevils striped in rainbow light.

The Magicians' Assistants

We met as I was placing my head
                 while nightly you felt knives
between the jaws of a lion,
          plotting your outline.

In the beginning we
        billed as twins
          toured in a caravan,
          with a mind-reading act.
                    finishing sentences
We saw our future in bone china,
                    girl-turned-tiger,
as doves from a cloche
          Aztec Lady, quartered.

Over the years
        you saw a magician   push a clean blade
                   through my boxed torso
(I kicked in encouragement,
stage light catching my legs).
        I have watched you climb a dizzy ladder
in ostrich feathers and fire
                a man from a cannon
                   with a shower of glitter.

We lost handcuffs, padlocks,
and straight-jackets,   left the sight
                    of fake smoke and astonishment.
Nowadays our conversation progresses
                    like silk from a dark sleeve
                    as we think back.

We smile at success
        as if we have never   pulled ties with our teeth,
                    crouched in a box,
                    felt the trapdoor.

Nowadays we thumb wine lists;
an illusion of indecision   (the waiters know our taste for
                    Montepulciano).
When we would invite the audience
to pick black   or red cards,
            the two of diamonds had a secret inevitability.
We do miss wearing blindfolds   as if ignorant of rhombi,
a diamond's carbonic origin,   a diamond's adamancy.

Bath time

For my sister

I had two years on you,
        adrift
in a great wet wash.

I slapped
        against the taps,
got lost hunting
        big fish soap,

soaked walls
        with slipping under.
Just me in a small ship

        all at sea.

So I call your little arms
        compass,
give your tiny legs
        the title *map*.

You delineated land,
steered true;

you understood
        north, south,
        sunrise
and occasional flags.

You helped me
          unknot the stars

and navigate
          to larger arms,
shore.

Snakebite

i.m. Helen Penfold, 1961-1999

Things are looking up. We've
found a pub where the landlord,
convinced by my smooth lies, your

proper breasts, will serve us snakebite.
He tips the lip of each pint glass,
froths in lager, pours cider and asks

How much blackcurrant, ladies?
You smile at him, murmur *When* –
we love how his hands shake

as you take your change.
We gulp like seasoned drinkers,
avoiding the stares of the old gits

with their bitter, their racing pages.
The drink hits the spot and
everything is funny. You nearly

take my eye out playing darts.
And at the Rec on the way home,
full of sugar and gas, we slump

on the swings we dared each other
to leap from as kids, jewelling
our palms and knees with grit.

———

We lean back under the night sky,
under all the stars we can't name,
we're full of how we'll leave

this dump of a town first chance we get –
how we despise the regular lawns,
the sagging paddling pools, we're

singing as we approach our road.
Today was hot, like the days,
buckling with laughter, we shoved

each other over on your drive,
the tarmac sucked at our sandals
and the ice-cream van played *Lara*

from *Dr. Zhivago*, too slow. Tomorrow
we'll feel sick as dogs. But tonight,
here, under a bright, full moon,

we're amazing, and as we hug
on my doorstep, I taste you,
kiss the snakebite off your lips.

I let your hand go

Agnosia

A girl watching a kiss at a party
from the kitchen window into the dark garden
an empty wine glass level in her loose hand
is here in London to see her friend
who arrived late, who left her
without sign or signal and who put on
yesterday's clothes and brought her here
and who looked unlike the girl from childhood
had forgotten how to measure a good dose
and whose accent was a famous song played backward
face an image flipped and printed out different
to the polaroids of the unbrushed girls
who had danced in school uniform
and later in black in undanceable shoes
in hometown bars, on hometown beaches
in the hometown home of their parents' homes
a girl who was cold, who wore the city like a coat
a girl she loved from the kitchen window
a girl who had clearly forgotten all they'd learned
who had forgotten how to say no
so the girl in the kitchen emptied her glass
and marched outside
and pulled the girl out of the kiss
and turned her round to look into her face
which was not her friend's face but a stranger's
and the music stopped
everybody looked at her
and a plane went overhead in the dark
and the wind took up all the dead leaves in the garden
and flung them back into the branches.

Catharsis

Dinner went well as we shared
  a mutual mistrust of clams and whelks
she told me about her herb garden so I volunteered
     my lifelong love of Euripides and she remarked
they'd never met but then said she adored
     August Kleinzahler and TS Eliot not to mention
Anne Carson and told me about the super-intelligent
Dachshund puppy she'd reserved on some licenced farm
    in Dorset who already obeyed commands without treats
    and I admit was still with the pedigree dogs
   those hanging bellies and inbred little legs when
  the conversation moved on to her daughter
who was apparently a bit touchy but not very
   and was taking elocution lessons so I said
  mine was learning the drums but didn't mention
   the tantrums which made it safe for her to invite us
    to the gîte in Bordeaux but the play was about to start
so we went to The Ladies well she called it The Ladies
   where we found we both wore the same shade
     Desert Plum which I took as a good sign
     especially as she offered me
a spray of Escada which felt quite intimate
    before asking me for the contact details of my
Australian hairdresser Bridget in Shoreditch
   and where she could get a copy of my little book
  and whether my daughter had Grade 8 piano
   yet because her daughter who quite honestly

cried too much had only just scraped
a Distinction which was surprising for a girl
who'd shown such promise she said
and I felt my eyes welling up but luckily
I don't think she noticed because by then
we were taking our seats and I thought about
how hard it is to make new friends once you reach
a certain age although I did remember to thank her for
choosing the play as the lights came up on
a run-down stately home with a sofa
where an old man in slippers entered stage left
and she whispered that she couldn't be doing with
The Greeks and thank God for Alan Bennett

Reconciliation

When all of this is over
and the floodwaters have
stonewashed the calico
of our lives with creases,

      I will cross the desert

where I have lived like O'Keeffe,
a basket of bones on my head
like a pile of braids

and my arms heavy
with a harvest of dark blooms
and bitter verdure.

There were so many things I wanted.
I didn't emerge transcendent.
I didn't come out of the forest
singing the poems.

But when I arrive at your door,
sun-bleached and bloodless,
with my skinned knees and my
face a dry saltern, allow me entry.
Allow me mercy.

Break bread with me, friend.
For the miles we put between us,
give me water.

Listening to The Streets

For Ella

I met you in the last year of cassettes.
We drank warm gin before Hall, radio shouting
You're listening to The Streets, your narrow room
hazy with late-spring heat and cigarettes

skinny as sugar twists, wisps of tobacco
and flecks of dope bound by a flat-broke lick,
then off we staggered through the sleeping bricks
to stand for Grace in tube tops and kimonos,

your hair purple and vertical, me with the cornrows
from that day you were bored. In the curry house
you bought me a rose. I stole your white shoes
and you stole a kiss at the ball you dressed me for,

I would remember that more than the notes
I slashed in books: 'Life: See page 73.'
We knew the world wanted us on our knees
but we stood proud in matching patent boots.

Our whole floor shook with canned R&B bands
mocking the choir. We thought we'd come so far
but all we knew were dresses, sweat and bars
and that was enough, then. We held uncertain hands

at the end, sat and wrote our names in beer,
watched them disappear into the sandstone
and rose together. At some point, I let your hand go
but I forget when. Part of me is still there.

Laura,

in the only photograph I have
of us, we're children on a carousel
with smiles that are the morning of
our trip to the London Eye. My
pointed feet, a promise of the night
we were to copy the Bolshoi in
front of the television. Your hair,
caught with the wind's hands, is
how I used to play with it. Mine,
cropped, is the feeling I had about
your first kiss. My teeth are showing.
Your closed mouth is a kept word.
The pole that spears the cartoon
horse. The people I don't know.

Night Shift, Burnham Deepdale

The Norfolk night is damson, still,
only the scratching
of your intermittent breath
frets at the silence.

Hours elide, shifts change, the doctor
shakes her head, says
you should have gone six weeks ago
but that now all bets are off.

Stay-at-home sister, these past weeks
you have slipped free
from the bed's iron-bars
to go travelling at last

but the journey's not been easy –
why, you whispered, did I leave you
in the desert without water,
on a mountain without food?

I lift back a strand of hair,
swab your lips, your blind eyes,
change sheets, replace the rosary
in your restless fingers.

Some things
we both know

The Tomato Salad

was breathtaking. Sometime in the late 1990s
the Californian sun ripened a crop of tomatoes
to such a pitch you could hear them screaming.
Did I mention this was in California? There was
corn on the cob. She was English and her heart
almost stopped when her aunt served her a bowl
of red and yellow tomatoes so spectacular she would
never get over them. I can only imagine the perfectly
suspended seeds, the things a cut tomato knows
about light, or in what fresh voice of sweet and tart
those tomatoes spoke when they told my dearest
friend, 'Yosçi yosçi lom boca sá tutty foo twa
tamata,' in the language of all sun-ripened fruits.

For Lois Lee

Dear Diary

I'd like to cut you up.
Dear Ms Walker, please don't read my diary.

That dream, I told to her on the walk to school.
That dream is a secret.

Dear diary, we dislike the word buds.
These, they tell us, are the beginning of breasts. Please

spare us the marshmallows over candles
or teenage pregnancy morality play

with 'Jump around' in, made up by Mr Smith.
I'd like to cut you up and turn you into something new.

Dear Buds, you are fucking awful. Diary,
they told us to be nice and quiet and here are some self-
    defense moves.

Yes we know we can't get pregnant from the foam pit
at Steel City Gym. But we might catch herpes.

Dear diary I am fucking a rabbit.
I'm lying. We hate you, and also we love you.

What we do after school is a secret, diary, I'm lying.
Trip hop is a thing, candles etc. We don't just paint nails.

She doesn't just fancy him,
I love him too but I will never, never tell you how, diary.

———

They held hands for one week. That was it.
We hold hands all the time.

She was thinking of writing
to that magazine to ask about pads for daily discharge.
  I was thinking how imaginative.

No I wasn't. And I lied about which tapes I like.
This week it is not Powder. We have practiced blowbacks.

No Henry Firth did not get off with everyone. i.e. I did
  not and never will get off with Henry Firth.

This is not mardiness. I'd like
not to have buds thank you very much.

I like mild trancy feeling. She likes mild trancy feeling.
We only took poppers once, I'm lying.

Why are we friends? Because of the word Luncheon.
Because of Helen of Troy and Michael Rosen.

Because she had weed. And we both liked competitive
  reading.
There were some things we both knew.

He made me try a cider lolly. Dear diary I am
  revealing it once
and for all, we didn't like *The Hobbit*, we only read it

to get ahead. And the lipstick poem
on the mirror was not us, though I wished it was.

We don't ever get into 'scrapes'.
They are not called 'scrapes'.

Dear Diary I never listened to the Powder tape. But
   I wanted to.
Fuck off, I'm lying.

Cut-Up Neighbour Mash-Up

Sorry to trouble you but
      In the future occasionally, if and when

I had no problem with it – but the only thing
      is also not a big deal – but here is the but:

Please be assured that I am not making this one up
      And here is another lesson I learned

And ringing my doorbell also shows
      I don't mean to be funny but Just a short

note to say Just to inform everyone that
      You have this rather unusual habit

I am sorry but I am not impressed I might look
      after your It is a bit annoying

'O God, 70, Can You Believe??
Come Over. No Cake.'

(For Rizzo On Her Birthday)

'Perhaps the frosting on the cake is too
pink. The lid slipped on the food dye
and I had no time to start again, besides
the colour scheme options are fixed –
it's not like even she would eat a cake
I'd buttercreamed in black – and who's to say
how pink is too pink anyway? Make sure
it's flat in the back, there. Don't squash it.
Please don't squash it more. Marty, sweet,
okay with me up front? Forget the seatbelt
if your stitches are sore – I'll go slow and skip
the bumps, and skip the black and whites
as well – but cops would never flag us down:
four old ladies in a beige sedan... I am
speaking for myself and old is what I say.
My new old lady pills arrived today. Blood,
heart, lungs, water – I got so many pills I sound
like a maraca. This time, truly, we are seniors.
And your week, French? Five years on Friday
since he went. It's the middle of the night
that brings it home the most. Two a.m.
three, four. You call. I'm here. We're here
and Lord, who's this one bursting out the door?
Betty's daughter's youngest, Little Riz –

—————————

who teethed on Jan's gold bangle, who's
on that porch step holding a pose as if
the blue night air itself should tune its pipes
and play the girl a song, who springs across
the lawn, who slaps our windshield with a high-five
and leaps on the back of a kerb-side bike,
who's a faint red brake-light and is gone.'

South Easterly

No, try again:
you know *full-well* I was drawn. Charcoal, eraser, rubbers and rubbing,
erasing, smudging and because of it – the tug of the skirt, a school of tights –
I conflated the other one with you, squinting with floaters at the strung-lights of
wilderness years and the compulsory wearing of double socks.

We tied shells to the veranda and called them Californian Hippie. I only recall
this because of the photograph left in the Swan Hotel, Gravesend.
The lipstick staining the grey flannel was *Siren*, downstairs it was 'Turkey and Tinsel'
in the dining hall, but, forgiving, they let us dance without shoes.

I hacked what we had with a cleaver flat-out on the chopping board your
sister bought us for our twenty-year friendship anniversary.
My only explanation – only, it isn't easy to explain – is that
you took a pirate ship to Valparaiso Bay but I couldn't follow you there.

Oh! Still, we are both in love with ports, rooms where prostitutes watch flies.
If I must, I will return to you the mirror letters shone upwards through
rock-pool reflection but, truly, the most we can hope for at this grave stage is
fresh sea-lettuce to hang a hook on, and the unlikeliest changeable weather.

No, try again:
you slept for seventeen years after dishing up your duty in plug holes.
I snapped a morning in Constantinople-Istanbul, then scratched out the
other people in the photo. If you like, it can be you, mistaking bait for a snack on
a low bridge in high wind, waving a glove at mackerel dying. It's simple enough to do.

The Wind and the Rain

The first time I asked her out she was in the Leisure Centre with an ex,

that's why she said No Way but she said it politely,

so I studied her in Geography. I made maps.

When I crossed the river to her house and fell in
she had to lend me her Dad's clothes.

Our wedding took place locally, she was pregnant at the time
and her dress had to be adjusted twice!

Everyone came, even Glen and Matthew Allen.

Sometimes when I lie in bed I hold my body very tense
then I think, why am I doing that? and I relax.

Joanna

After school in cupboard light
on the quilt sets of their master rooms
we practised on that broad toy clown
its face a bad-egg colour.

Christ hung around her neck
on a cubic zirconia cross.
Our parents make us suffer,
I would say to her, quite hot.

Homecoming

We meet again in the park: helmets on turnstiles,
fags put out against the snout of the sprung horse.
You sit on the saddle, cross your fake crocodile
boots. I hunch my back to hide my height.

No paste can hide the constellations on my nose,
your lips are the colour of a prune past its date.
You roll a joint like a tune, light up, shift weight
– your legs open, a smile playing at your lips.

The group drops like bin bags on the swings.
I scrape the varnish off my nails and recall,
'best friend', how your teeth typewrote with
the cold our tales: you made music from strings.

I am the underlined blank in your sentences;
my eyes are blue and yours are getting browner.

1989

Rich best friends steal key rings from desk drawers and P.E. is a race to be ready first so I wear shorts under my skirt. And when Anna wins one Wednesday I slow to a mechanical fail, a forever-loading webpage. These girls have tennis instructors whose own injuries prevent professional greatness. I have Holly Hobbie, a Muppet Babies duvet, every Kylie cassette, a tape deck and Disney videos wearing to static. I beat all exam scores but can't win Charlotte's favour and the McDonald's toys she chucks like wrappers, I queue for. She keeps back every character Kim wants. She's savouring some for Ally. I lucky-dip her discard plastic sack, then lean on the playground altar, eyeing Mary's immaculate stomach, and I wonder who will die first. I Sellotape the rosary cross Mrs Mitchell gave me, because it snapped, spinning, and I start my prayers, finish in time for pick up and Mum stops for chocolate at the Spar shop and this happens until 1994.

Stars of the County Down

Your hair is coming undone
like a frayed sleeve, and I
am so tired I'm seeing
dancing skeletons. It is
three a.m., and we have
always declined
the capable sweetness
of female friendship.
I'm not the kind to print
kisses, and you
disdain picnics of all sizes.

We don't sob on each other,
our tears falling out of us
in folksy faux doubloons;
we've never studied
heartbreak's bedside manner,
how to act when the mouth
is a crushed pout and *all
men are bastards.*

Our grandmothers had the hoary
hairshirt goodness of redoubtable
hags; had green flags and strong
tea, grim thrift and sensible shoes,
all reproachful cleanliness. But we
have no taste for piety; we are BacoFoil
bonkers, trouncing scalps in demon heels!

We're *mad as a box of frogs*. You're in
leather, I'm in leopard, and if there won't
be dancing, then it's not our revolution.

What we share, at three a.m.,
is the made face coming apart
in globs and daubs; is the bone-
idle bleakness of our border town
after the pubs have shut, and we
are forced to drink coffee and shots
in your grimy kitchen.

You grind out your cigarettes
with trashy aplomb, and swing
your foot into my lap: *my sole
is coming away!* you say.
For a moment I'm confused by that.

Christmas Eve

Tonight the Black Country is tinselled by sleet
falling on the little towns lit up in the darkness
like constellations – the Pigeon, the Collier –
and upon the shooting stars of boy racers
who comet through the streets in white Novas.
It's blowing in drifts from the pit banks,
over the brown ribbon of the cut, over Beacon Hill,
through the lap-loved chimneys of the factories.
Sleet is tumbling into the lap of the plastercast Mary
by the manger at St Jude's, her face gorgeous and naive
as the last Bilston carnival queen.
In the low-rise flats opposite the cemetery,
Mrs Showell is turning on her fibre-optic tree
and unfolding her ticket for the rollover lottery
though we ay never 'ad a bit o luck in ower lives
and upstairs in the box-rooms of a thousand semis
hearts are stuttering and minds unravelling
like unfinished knitting.
And the sleet fattens and softens to snow,
blanking the crowded rows of terraces
and their tiny hankies of garden, white now, surrendering
their birdfeeders and sandpits, the shed Mick built
last Autumn when the factory clammed up.
And the work's gone again
and the old boys are up at dawn to clock-on nowhere
except walk their dogs and sigh
at the cars streaming to call centres and supermarkets
because there ay nuthin in it that's mon's werk,

really bab, there ay...
But it's coming down now, really coming
over the stands at the Molineux, over Billy Wright
kicking his dreams into the ring road
and in the dark behind the mechanics
the O'Feeney's boy props his BMX against the lock-ups
and unzips to piss a flower into the snow
well gi' me strength Lord, to turn the other cheek
fer we'm the only ones half way decent round ere
and the tower blocks are advent calendars,
every curtain pulled to reveal a snow-blurred face.
And it's Christmas soon, abide it or not,
for now the pubs are illuminated pink and gold
The Crooked House, Ma Pardoes, The Struggling Mon
and snow is filling women's hair like blossom
and someone is drunk already and throwing a punch
and someone is jamming a key in a changed lock
shouting *for christ's sake, Myra, yo'll freeze me to jeth*
and a hundred new bikes are being wrapped in sheets
and small pyjamas warmed on fireguards
and children are saying *one more minute, just one, Mom*
and the old girls are watching someone die on a soap
and feeling every snow they've ever seen set in their bones.
It's snowing on us all
and I think of you, Eloise, down there in your terrace,
feeding your baby or touching his hand to the snow
and although we can't ever go back or be what we were
I can tell you, honestly, I'd give up everything I've worked for
or thought I wanted in this life,
to be with you tonight.

About the editor

Amy Key was born in Dover and grew up in Kent and the North East. She now lives and works in London. She co-edits the online journal *Poems in Which*. Her pamphlet *Instead of Stars* was published by tall-lighthouse press in 2009. Her debut collection *Luxe* was published by Salt in November 2013.

About the illustrator

Emma Wright worked in ebook production at Orion Publishing Group before leaving to found the Emma Press in 2012 with the support of the Prince's Trust Explore Enterprise programme. She lives in Birmingham.

Acknowledgements

'Will You Be My Friend, Kate Moss?', by Kathryn Maris, was first published in *Poetry London* and then in her collection *God Loves You* (Seren, 2013).

'Ute', by Annie Freud, was previously published in her collection *The Mirabelles* (Picador, 2010).

'I Want To Be In Your Gang', by Andrea Quinlan, was previously published in a different form in *Girls Get Busy* zine.

'Offchurch', by Holly Hopkins, first appeared in *Poetry Review* and has also been published in *Cast: The Poetry Business Book of New Contemporary Poets* (Smith/Doorstop, 2014), *Bedford Square 7* (Ward Wood Publishing, 2014) and her pamphlet *Soon Every House Will Have One* (Smith/Doorstop, 2014).

'Hot Corona', by Sophie Collins, was previously published in *I Love Roses When They're Past Their Best* (Test Centre, 2014).

'I Wish I Had More Sisters', by Brenda Shaughnessy, was first published in the *New Yorker* in 2010 and then in her collection *Our Andromeda* (Copper Canyon Press, 2012). Reprinted by permission of Copper Canyon Press.

'Snakebite', by Catherine Smith, was first published in her collection *Lip* (Smith/Doorstop, 2008).

'Night Shift, Burnham Deepdale', by Angela Kirby, was previously published in *Magma* in 2013, as well as in *A Scent of Winter* (Shoestring Press, 2013).

'The Tomato Salad', by Emily Berry, was previously published in her collection *Dear Boy* (Faber & Faber, 2013).

'The Wind and the Rain', by Megan Watkins, was previously published in *Poetry Wales* in 2014.

'Joanna', by Rachael Allen, was previously published in *The Poetry Review* in 2014.

'Homecoming', by Claire Trévien, was previously published in *Low-Tide Lottery* (Salt, 2011).

'Christmas Eve', by Liz Berry, was first published in *The North* magazine in 2013 and then in her collection *Black Country* (Chatto & Windus, 2014). Reprinted by permission of The Random House Group Limited.

About the poets

Rachael Allen is co-editor of poetry anthology series *Clinic* and online journal *tender*. A pamphlet of her poems has been published by Faber as part of the Faber New Poets series.

Emily Berry is a poet, writer and editor. Her debut poetry collection *Dear Boy* (Faber & Faber, 2013) won the Forward Prize for Best First Collection (2013) and the Hawthornden Prize (2014).

Liz Berry was born in the Black Country and now lives in Birmingham. She received an Eric Gregory Award, an Arvon-Jerwood mentorship and won the *Poetry London* competition in 2012. Her debut collection, *Black Country* (Chatto, 2014), was a PBS Recommendation and won the Forward Prize for Best First Collection.

Julia Bird grew up in Gloucestershire and now lives in London, where she works for the Poetry School and as an independent live literature producer. She has published two collections – *Hannah and the Monk* (Salt, 2008) and *Twenty-Four Seven Blossom* (Salt, 2013).

Sophia Blackwell's debut collection, *Into Temptation*, was published in 2009 and a novel, *After My Own Heart*, in 2012. She has been published in *Rising, Fuselit, Diva* and *Time Out.*

Sophie Collins is co-founder of *tender*, an online quarterly promoting work by female-identified writers and artists. Her poems and translations have been published in *Poetry, Poetry London, Oxford Poetry*, and elsewhere. In 2014 she received an Eric Gregory Award.

Nia Davies is a poet and editor. Her pamphlet of poems *Then spree* came out in 2012 from Salt. She edits *Poetry Wales* and co-edits *Poems in Which*. Her next publication is a chapbook: *Çekoslovakyalılaştıramadıklarımızdanmısınız or Long words*.

Francine Elena's chapbook *Christmas Lantern* is published by 3:AM Press. Her poems have appeared in the *Best British Poetry 2013* and *Furies* anthologies as well as *Clinic, 3:AM Magazine, Poems in Which* and *The Quietus* among others.

Annie Freud's first full poetry collection, *The Best Man That Ever Was* (Picador, 2007), was awarded the Dimplex Prize for New Writing (Poetry). Her second collection, *The Mirabelles* (Picador, 2010), was shortlisted for the TS Eliot Prize. Her third collection, *The Remains*, was published in 2015. She is also an artist and teaches poetry composition.

Sophie Herxheimer is an artist and a poet, interested in text, image, collaboration and performance. She's held numerous residencies (e.g. for London International Festival of Theatre, Transport for London) and is currently making a book in a forest for Fermynwoods Contemporary Art. Her work has been exhibited and published widely.

Holly Hopkins lives in London. She won an Eric Gregory Award in 2011 and her debut pamphlet, *Soon Every House Will Have One*, won the 2014 Poetry Business Pamphlet Competition and was Poetry Book Society Pamphlet Choice.

Emma Jeremy was born in Bristol and is currently based in London working towards a Masters degree in Creative Writing. Her work has appeared in *Rising, Poems in Which* and *The Voices Inside Our Heads*.

Suzanne Joinson is a novelist, poet and non-fiction writer. Her debut novel, *A Lady Cyclist's Guide to Kashgar*, was published by Bloomsbury in 2012. In 2007 she won the New Writing Ventures Award for her short story 'Leila Ahmed'. She writes for a range of publications and lives by the sea in Sussex.

Angela Kirby's poems have been translated into Romanian, performed on BBC Television and Radio Four and won several prizes and commendations including BBC Wildlife Poet of the Year in 1995 and 2001. She has published three collections with Shoestring Press: *Mr Irresistible* (2004), *Dirty Work* (2008) and *The Scent of Winter* (2013).

Fran Lock is a sometime itinerant dog whisperer and poet, now living and working in London. Her debut collection *Flatrock* (Little Episodes) was published in 2011 and her second collection *The Mystic and The Pig Thief* (Salt) was published in 2014.

Amy Mackelden lives in Newcastle upon Tyne. She won a Northern Promise Award from New Writing North in 2011 and co-founded northern poetry magazine *Butcher's Dog*. She co-edits Feminist Trash TV blog *Clarissa Explains Fuck All*, and is working on her first collection.

Sharanya Manivannan is the author of a book of poems, *Witchcraft* (Bullfighter Books, 2008). Her poetry, fiction and essays have appeared in *Hobart, Wasafiri, Drunken Boat, Prairie Schooner, Killing The Buddha* and elsewhere. She has received an Elle Fiction Award and a Lavanya Sankaran Fellowship. She lives in India.

Kathryn Maris is from New York City. She lives in London, where she teaches creative writing and writes essays and reviews. *God Loves You* (Seren) was published in 2013 and is her second collection of poems.

Karen McCarthy Woolf is the recipient of an Arts and Humanities Research Council scholarship from Royal Holloway, where she is a PhD candidate. She has edited three anthologies, most recently *Ten: The New Wave* (Bloodaxe, 2014), and her collection *An Aviary of Small Birds* (Carcanet, 2014) is a Poetry Book Society Recommendation.

Rebecca Perry is a graduate of Manchester's Centre for New Writing. She has had work published in *Poetry London, The Quietus* and *Best British Poetry 2013*. Her pamphlet, *little armoured* (Seren), and was a Poetry Book Society Pamphlet Choice. Her first full collection, *Beauty/Beauty*, was published by Bloodaxe in 2015.

Rachel Piercey is an editor at *The Cadaverine* magazine and the Emma Press. Her illustrated pamphlet of love poems, *The Flower and the Plough*, was published by the Emma Press in 2013 and her second pamphlet, *Rivers Wanted*, was published in 2014.

Kathy Pimlott grew up in Nottingham but has lived in London for the last forty years, most of that time in Seven Dials, where she looks after bollards and street signs. Her poems have appeared in *Magma, The North, South Bank Poetry* and *Mslexia*.

Andrea Quinlan is a poet and writer based in New Zealand. Her chapbook *We Speak Girl* was published by Dancing Girl Press in 2012 and *The Mysteries of Laura* was published by Birds of Lace in 2013. She has been published in *brief, Gaga Stigmata, Delirious Hem, NNATAN* and *Finery*.

Jacqueline Saphra's first full collection, *The Kitchen of Lovely Contraptions* (flipped eye), was developed with funding from Arts Council England and nominated for The Aldeburgh First Collection Prize 2012. Her illustrated book of prose poems, *If I Lay on my Back I saw Nothing but Naked Women*, was published by the Emma Press in 2014.

Brenda Shaughnessy is the author of *Our Andromeda, Human Dark with Sugar* and *Interior with Sudden Joy*. Her poems have been published in *Best American Poetry, The New Yorker, Paris Review* and *McSweeney's*. A 2013 Guggenheim Fellow, she teaches at Rutgers-Newark and lives in Brooklyn with her family.

Two of **Catherine Smith**'s poetry collections, *The New Bride* and *Lip*, have been shortlisted for Forward Prizes. In 2004, she was included in the PBS/Arts Council 'Next Generation' promotion and in Mslexia's 'Best Ten New Women Poets'. Her latest poetry project, *The Ballad of the New Cockaigne*, was published by Pighog in 2014.

Martha Sprackland lives in London by way of Merseyside and Madrid. Work has appeared in *Poetry Review*, the *London Review of Books* and *Poetry London*, amongst others. She was co-founder and poetry editor of *Cake* magazine, and is Assistant Poetry Editor at Faber & Faber. In 2014 she won an Eric Gregory Award.

Camellia Stafford was born in Warwickshire. Her debut pamphlet, *another pretty colour, another break for air* is published by tall lighthouse and *Letters to the Sky*, her first collection, is published by Salt. Camellia works in museum education.

Claire Trévien is the author of *Low-Tide Lottery* (Salt, 2011) and *The Shipwrecked House* (Penned in the Margins, 2013), which was longlisted in the Guardian First Book Awards.

Megan Watkins works part-time at the Royal Academy and writes poetry. She is a contributor to various magazines and was featured in *The Emma Press Anthology of Motherhood*. She often collaborates with her friend the artist and writer Audrey Reynolds. She has two children, a cat and a hamster.

Laura Webb was born in 1985. She recently completed a PhD about Ted Hughes at Sheffield University. Amongst other places, she has had poems published in *CAST: The Poetry Business Book of New Contemporary Poets*, *Poetry Ireland Review*, *The Manchester Review*, *Stand* and *The Rialto*. She works for an education charity.

Alison Winch has published in *Rialto* 75 and *Poems in Which* 3 and 5, among others. She was featured poet in *Magma* 52 and is currently working on her first collection. She has published nonfiction work, including *Girlfriends* (Palgrave 2014). She is based in London.

ABOUT THE EMMA PRESS

small press, big dreams

☙❧

The Emma Press is an independent publisher dedicated to producing beautiful, thought-provoking books. It was founded in 2012 by Emma Wright in Winnersh and is now based in the Jewellery Quarter, Birmingham.

Having been shortlisted in both 2014 and 2015, the Emma Press was awarded the Michael Marks Award for Poetry Pamphlet Publishers in 2016.

The Emma Press is passionate about publishing literature which is welcoming and accessible. Sign up to the Emma Press newsletter to hear about upcoming events, publications and calls for submissions.

theemmapress.com
emmavalleypress.blogspot.co.uk

MILDLY EROTIC VERSE

Edited by Rachel Piercey and Emma Wright
RRP £10 / ISBN 978-1-910139-34-9

Mildly Erotic Verse skips the mechanics and dives straight into the emotional core of sex, celebrating the diversity and eccentricity of human sexuality.

POSTCARD STORIES

Stories by Jan Carson, illustrated by Benjamin Phillips
RRP £6.50 / ISBN 978-1-910139-68-4

Every day in 2015, Jan Carson wrote a short story on the back of a postcard and mailed it to a friend. Each of these tiny stories was inspired by an event, an overheard conversation, a piece of art or just a glance of something worth thinking about further.

FIRST FOX

Stories by Leanne Radojkovich, illustrated by Rachel J Fenton
RRP £6.50 / ISBN 978-1-910139-70-7

The stories in *First fox* offer an everyday world tinged with the dreamlike qualities of fairy tales. Disappointments and consolations meet with fantastical moments, winding their way into the realm of possibility.

ALSO FROM THE EMMA PRESS

Now You Can Look

Poems by Julia Bird, illustrated by Anna Vaivare
RRP £10 / ISBN 978-1-910139-84-4

This is a tale you can read three ways. The first time through, it's the story of a woman who takes one glance at conventional early-twentieth-century life, and throws in her lot with art instead.

Dragonish

Poems by Emma Simon, introduced by Caroline Bird
RRP £6.50 / ISBN 978-1-910139-64-6

Loss, love and various severed body parts are scattered throughout *Dragonish*. The poems are rooted in family, friends and home while also reaching into other worlds: the circus of possibilities, an earth-bound heavenly host, London's dryads and a nineteenth-century French brothel.

The Secret Box

Stories by Daina Tabūna, translated by Jayde Will
RRP £6.50 / ISBN 9-78-1-910139-90-5

On the cusp of womanhood, Daina Tabūna's heroines are constantly confronted with the unexpected. Adult life seems just around the corner, but so are the kinds of surprise encounter which might change everything.

ALSO FROM THE EMMA PRESS

PAISLEY

Poems by Rakhshan Rizwan, introduced by Leila Aboulela
RRP £6.50 / ISBN 978-1-910139-78-3

Drawing on the rich visual and material culture of her home region, Rizwan unpacks and offers critical comment on the vexed issues of class, linguistic and cultural identity – particularly for women – in the context of Pakistan and South Asia.

THE EMMA PRESS ANTHOLOGY OF AUNTS

Edited by Rachel Piercey and Emma Wright
RRP £10 / ISBN 978-1-910139-66-0

The *Anthology of Aunts* explores what it means to be – and feels like to have – an aunt, historically and today. Some aunts are biological, some are chosen, but all have an impact on the way we learn to move through the world.

THE EMMA PRESS ANTHOLOGY OF THE SEA

Edited by Eve Lacey
RRP £10 / ISBN 978-1-910139-45-5

In the *Anthology of the Sea*, poets ask how the human mind can fathom the ocean's depths. The sea emerges as at once strange and familiar, bearing witness to storms, ocean creatures and the human desire for freedom.